EDGE BOOKS

BMX EXTREME

BMX GREATS

by Brian D. Fiske

Consultant:
Keith Mulligan
Editor/Photographer
TransWorld BMX Magazine

Capstone press

Mankato, Minnesota

Edge Books are published by Capstone Press
151 Good Counsel Drive, P.O. Box 669, Mankato, Minnesota 56002
www.capstonepress.com

Library of Congress Cataloging-in-Publication Data
Fiske, Brian D.
  BMX greats / by Brian D. Fiske.
  p. cm.—(Edge books. BMX extreme)
  Includes bibliographical references and index.
  Contents: Beginner to pro—BMX founders—Early greats—Today's greats.
  ISBN 0-7368-2434-0 (hardcover)
  1. Bicycle motocross—Juvenile literature. 2. Cyclists—United States—
Biography—Juvenile literature. [1. Bicycle motocross. 2. Bicycle racing.] I. Title.
II. Series.
GV1049.3.F58 2004
796.6'2—dc22   2003013711

Editorial Credits
Angela Kaelberer, editor; Enoch Peterson, series designer; Jason Knudson,
    book designer; Jo Miller, photo researcher

Photo Credits
Getty Images/Elsa, 29; Mark Mainz, 24
James Cassimus, 12
Keith Mulligan/TransWorld BMX, 6, 18, 19, 20, 23, 28
Scot "OM" Breithaupt, 11
SportsChrome-USA/Rob Tringali Jr., cover, 5, 8, 26
Tim Lillethorup, 15, 16, 17

Table of Contents

CHAPTER 1

Beginner to Pro

At the 2002 Summer X Games, Mat Hoffman did something that had never been done before. In the middle of his run, Hoffman aired out of the halfpipe. He began rotating and threw his hands out to his sides. After two and one-half spins, Hoffman put his hands back on the handlebars as his wheels touched the ramp. The fans, announcers, and other riders were amazed by Hoffman's no-handed 900. A crash later in his run kept Hoffman from winning the vert event, but he still came in second.

At that moment, thousands of BMX riders wanted to be like Hoffman. He was a pro rider who achieved something nobody else had done. But he started out as a kid on a bike, just like everyone else.

Learn about:

- Skill levels
- Amateurs and pros
- Sponsorship

Mat Hoffman has competed in
pro events since the 1980s.

Less experienced riders compete in amateur classes.

Competition Levels

BMX riders can compete in races or freestyle events. Freestyle riders do tricks on their bikes. Judges give them scores based on their performance and the difficulty of their tricks.

Racers first compete in the amateur class. This class includes three skill levels. Beginning racers compete at the novice level. As riders gain experience, they move to the intermediate level. Expert is the highest amateur level.

The top riders race in the pro classes. Pro riders first race in the A class. The top riders move up to the AA class. Only a few riders have the skill, experience, and confidence to race at this level.

Both amateur and pro riders compete for prize money. Pro riders usually compete in more events than amateurs do. Pro riders earn a living from competing. Most amateur riders have other jobs or are still in school.

Riders wear their sponsors' logos on their clothing and helmets.

8

Sponsored Riders

Many top amateur and pro riders are sponsored. Companies give them bikes, parts, or money to help them compete. In return, riders place the company's name or logo on their bikes or clothing. They also may appear in advertisements or TV commercials for the company's products.

Companies want to see what a rider can do for them before they agree to a sponsorship. Riders who want to become sponsored should first write a résumé. A résumé is a summary of the rider's skills and achievements. Along with the résumé, some freestyle riders send a videotape that shows their best tricks. Riders call this tape a "sponsor-me" video. A rider who does well in events and who can spread excitement about a company's products has a good chance of being sponsored.

BMX Founders

Several people played important roles in the early days of BMX. These people helped start the sport and make it popular.

The Old Man

Many people consider Scot Breithaupt the founder of BMX. Even when he was a teenager, people called him the "old man" of the sport.

In 1970, 14-year-old Breithaupt raced motorcycles in his hometown of Long Beach, California. He saw some kids riding bicycles on the track where he practiced and decided to have a race. Breithaupt divided the 30 riders into skill levels. He gave some of his motorcycle trophies to the winners. The next week, 150 racers came.

Learn about:

- **Scot Breithaupt**
- **Bob Haro**
- **R. L. Osborn**

Scot Breithaupt organized some of the first BMX races.

Breithaupt competed in pro races until the late 1980s. He also started his own bike company, SE Racing. Today, Breithaupt owns a loan company. He sometimes races in events for riders age 40 and older.

Bob Haro was one of the first riders to do tricks on halfpipe ramps.

First Freestyle Riders

In the 1970s, Bob Haro was a talented rider and artist. His artwork appeared in BMX newspapers and magazines.

Haro started doing tricks with his bike at skateparks in the mid-1970s. In 1979, Haro teamed with R. L. Osborn to form the *BMX ACTION* Trick Team, sponsored by *BMX ACTION* magazine. Haro and Osborn were among the first riders to do tricks on halfpipe ramps, in skateparks, and on flat ground. They jumped over cars, trucks, and people.

After two years, Haro left the team. In 1980, he started his own company, Haro Designs. This company is now Haro Bicycle Corporation. Haro sold the company in 1988. Today, he owns a graphic design company.

CHAPTER 3

Early Greats

BMX became even more popular during the late 1970s and early 1980s. New riders pushed the limits of the sport, making it faster and more exciting.

Stompin' Stu

Stu Thomsen was one of the first BMX racing stars. In 1974, 16-year-old Thomsen competed in the first large BMX race series. The Yamaha Gold Cup Series was a group of races held in California. Thomsen won the Gold Cup championship race in the expert class. In 1979, he became the first American Bicycle Association (ABA) National Pro champion.

Learn about:

- Stu Thomsen
- Dave Clinton
- Greg Hill

Stu Thomsen (#27) was one of the first BMX racing stars.

In 1978, Shimano Bikes was Dave Clinton's sponsor.

Thomsen's nickname was "Stompin' Stu." People called him that because he won so many races. By the mid-1980s, he was earning more money from racing and sponsorships than any other rider. Today, he is a member of both the ABA BMX Hall of Fame and the U.S. Bicycling Hall of Fame.

Dynamite Dave

Dave Clinton also was a top rider in the 1970s. In 1971, he started racing at age 11 in California. He turned pro three years later.

Clinton is known for doing many things first. He was the first rider sponsored by a large manufacturer, Kawasaki. In 1974, he invented one of the first BMX tricks, the tabletop. In 1975, he won the first National Bicycle Association championship. Ten years later, he became the first member of the ABA BMX Hall of Fame.

Dave Clinton (#13) often left other riders in the dust.

Gary Ellis

Gary Ellis had one of the longest and most successful careers in BMX racing. He started racing in 1977 at age 11. At age 18, he turned pro. He won the ABA No. 1 Pro title in 1989, 1990, 1994, and 1995. In 1998, Ellis retired from racing. He later became manager of Nirve Bicycles' racing team.

Greg Hill

In the 1980s, Greg Hill was one of the top BMX riders in the world. Hill started racing on a Schwinn Stingray in 1974 at age 11.

Gary Ellis' (#220) racing career lasted 21 years.

Greg Hill is a five-time
Pro World champion.

In 1982, Hill won his first Pro World
championship. In 1983, Hill started a bike
company, Greg Hill Products (GHP). He won
four more Pro World titles during the 1980s.

Hill retired from pro racing in 1989. Today,
he teaches young people about BMX riding.

Kim Hayashi is one of the best female racers.

Women in BMX

Not all of the top BMX riders are men. Many girls and women also have done well in the sport.

Cindy Davis is one of the best-known female racers. Between 1988 and 1995, Davis won two ABA National Girl Pro titles and three ABA National Girl Cruiser titles. She was the first rider to win five ABA World Cup titles in a row. In 1998, Davis retired from racing with 350 national wins.

Today, Kim Hayashi is one of the best female BMX riders. Hayashi won the 2000 ABA National Girl Cruiser title at age 14. She won the title again the next year.

Today's Greats

Racers were the stars in the early years of BMX. Since the mid-1990s, freestyle riders have received most of the fans' attention.

Freestyle riders compete in four events. In vert events, riders do tricks off halfpipe ramps. Park riders do tricks on courses with ramps of various sizes. Flatland riders do tricks on flat, paved surfaces. Dirt riders jump their bikes over mounds of dirt called doubles.

In 2001, the X Games added downhill BMX races. Riders race down hills that have big jumps and banked turns called berms. Downhill tracks are about 1,500 feet (460 meters) long.

Learn about:

- **Dave Mirra**
- **Mat Hoffman**
- **New stars**

Ryan Nyquist is one of today's top freestyle riders.

Dave Mirra has won more X Games medals than any other BMX rider.

The Miracle Boy

Dave Mirra has been one of the best-known freestyle riders since the late 1980s. People call him "Miracle Boy" because of his daring moves.

Mirra started riding in 1978 at age 4. He competed in his first freestyle contest when he was 10. Mirra placed second to last, but he kept practicing. By age 13, he was good enough to ride for Haro.

Mirra competes in park and vert events. In 2000, he became the first rider to do a double backflip in competition.

Mat Hoffman has invented at least 100 freestyle tricks.

PROVIDENCE PROVIDENCE PROVIDENCE
RHODE ISLAND   RHODE ISLAND   RHODE ISLAND

PROVIDENCE, R.I.

Mat Hoffman

Many people consider Mat Hoffman the greatest vert rider in BMX history. Hoffman has won nearly every vert championship that exists. He invented the flair, the flip fakie, and at least 100 other tricks.

Hoffman started competing in freestyle events in 1983 at age 13. Three years later, he turned pro. At 19, he started his own bike company. Today, he splits his time between competing and running Hoffman Bikes.

Stars of the Future

Every year, new riders move up from the amateur level to the pro classes. Some of these riders become stars of the sport.

Ryan Nyquist started riding in 1991 at age 12. Many freestyle riders focus on one event, but Nyquist competes in dirt, park, and vert. In 2002, he won the park gold medal at the X Games. In 2003, he won X Games gold in both park and dirt.

Chad Kagy also competes in dirt, park, and vert. He started riding in 1988 at age 10. In 1994, he turned pro. In 2002, he won the bronze medal in park at the X Games.

Koji Kraft is one of the youngest new BMX stars. He competes in both park and vert events. Kraft was born in 1982 and started riding at age 11. He rides with Mat Hoffman on the Hoffman Bikes team.

Some BMX fans compare Koji Kraft's style to Mat Hoffman's.

Besides vert, Chad Kagy also competes in park and dirt events.

BMX riders often have longer careers than athletes who compete in other extreme sports. Many riders stay involved in the sport in some way even after they retire. Their experience and skill helps train the stars of the future.

Glossary

amateur (AM-uh-chur)—an athlete who usually does not earn a living from competing in a sport

berm (BURM)—a banked turn or corner on a BMX track

freestyle (FREE-stile)—a type of BMX riding that focuses on tricks and jumps

novice (NOV-iss)—a competitive class for beginning amateur riders

résumé (RE-zuh-may)—a written summary of an athlete's achievements

sponsor (SPON-sur)—a business that helps pay an athlete's expenses; athletes use and help advertise the sponsor's products in return.

vert (VURT)—a style of BMX riding done on large ramps called halfpipes

Read More

Blomquist, Christopher. *BMX in the X Games.* Kid's Guide to the X Games. New York: PowerKids Press, 2003.

Nelson, Julie. *BMX Racing and Freestyle.* Extreme Sports. Austin, Texas: Steadwell Books, 2002.

Parr, Danny. *Extreme Bicycle Stunt Riding Moves.* Behind the Moves. Mankato, Minn.: Capstone Press, 2001.

Useful Addresses

American Bicycle Association
P.O. Box 718
Chandler, AZ 85244

National Bicycle League
3958 Brown Park Drive, Suite D
Hilliard, OH 43026

TransWorld BMX
1421 Edinger Avenue, Suite D
Tustin, CA 92780

Internet Sites

FactHound offers a safe, fun way to find Internet sites related to this book. All of the sites on FactHound have been researched by our staff.

Here's how:

1. Visit *www.facthound.com*
2. Type in this special code **0736824340** for age-appropriate sites. Or enter a search word related to this book for a more general search.
3. Click on the **Fetch It** button.

FactHound will fetch the best sites for you!

Index